# Colorful
# Creatures

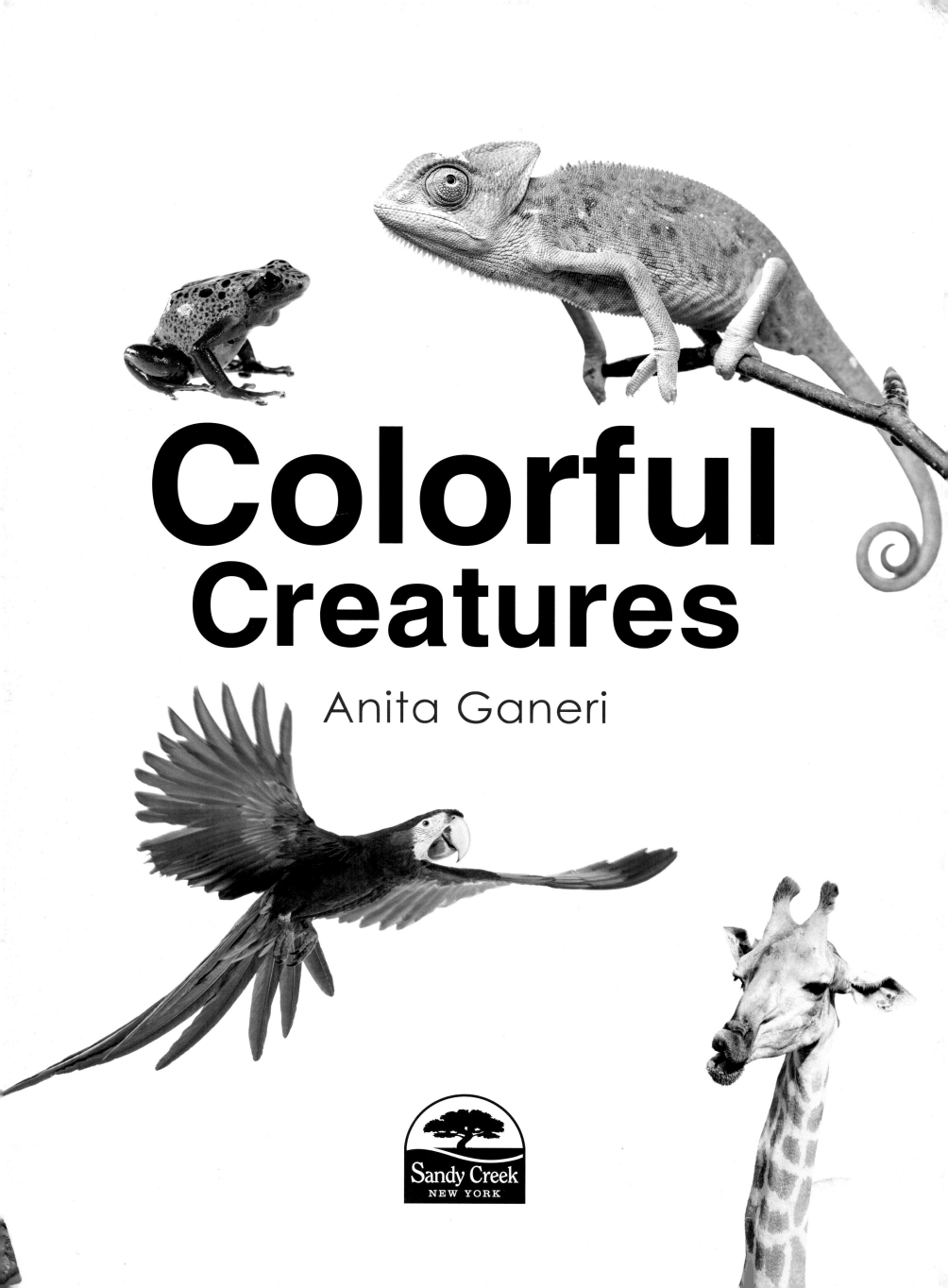

# Colorful
# Creatures

Anita Ganeri

Sandy Creek
NEW YORK

An Imprint of Sterling Publishing Co., Inc.
1166 Avenue of the Americas
New York, NY 10036

ISBN 978-1-4351-6383-6

Manufactured in Guangdong, China.
Lot#:
2 4 6 8 10 9 7 5 3 1
05/16

# Contents

# Hello Color

Red, yellow, brown, pink, purple, blue, and orange—animals come in all sorts of colors. Some animals are brightly colored while other animals are harder to spot. Their colors are not simply for showing off. In nature, colors and patterns help animals to stay alive.

Some colors help animals to blend into the background for protection. While certain colors help animals to send signals to each other. This allows the animals to keep in touch and even find a mate. Bright colors are often warning signs that an animal tastes horrible or is poisonous.

Many animals have more than one color or pattern. They may be multicolored or have mixtures of stripes, splotches, and spots. These markings look strong and striking, but they also confuse attackers who find the animals difficult to see and catch. A few animals can even change color so that they can hide in different places, and also show their feelings.

In this book, you will meet animals of many colors, from striking black-and-white zebras to stunning emerald-green lizards. See if you can guess what they use their colors for.

# Red

Many insects use mimicry to hide from predators or attract prey. This means they pretend to be something that they are not—like a disguise! The red leaf beetle, for example, is not poisonous, but a bird might avoid eating it because it looks similar to the poisonous ladybug.

Ladybugs

Grouper fish

Butterfly

Dart frog

Golden
net-wing
beetles

Scarlet lily beetle

Butterfly

Indonesian
beetles

Butterfly

Milksnake

Butterfly

Red velvet mites

Bamboo snake

Firebug

Calico snake

Cardinal

Crab

Moontail bullseye fish

Seed tick

Bigeye fish

Palm weevils

Betta fish

Bigeye fish

Australian
king parrot

Indonesian
beetle

Potato
beetle

Sea star

Scarlet ibis

Scarlet
lily
beetle

Parrotfish

Ladybug

Stonefish

Betta fish

Cardinal
lory

Sea star

Cichlid fish

Scarlet ibis

Butterfly

Red velvet mites

Seed ticks

Ladybird spider

Sea star

Bullfinch

Rooster

Red squirrel

Velvet ant

Betta fish

Strawberry finch

Bullfinch

Ark clams

Bearded dragons

Scallops

Monkfish

Great frigatebird

Velvet ants

Colorado beetles

Betta fish

Milksnake

Turkey

Sharp-nosed
crab

Stag beetle

Hermit crab

Lady beetles

Cardinal

Tomato frog

Yellow-bibbed
lory

Macaw

Panther chameleon

Firebugs

Butterfly

Mandrill

Coral snake

Poplar leaf beetle

Red snappers

Sockeye
salmon

# Orange

Orange animals, such as Monarch butterflies, are easy to spot. But their bright color sends a message to hungry birds. It tells them to stay away—these butterflies are horrible to eat.

Sea stars

Corn snake

Sea slug

Sea urchin

Gila lizard

Cat

Grasshoppers

Orangutan

Newts

Tomato frog

Slug

Crab

Clownfish

Caterpillar

Monarch butterflies

Llama

Stag beetle

Atlas moth

Cock-of-the-rock

Tiger

Butterflies

Discus fish

Kitten

Bearded dragon

Tarantula

Scorpion

Hummingbird

Parakeets

Goldfish

17

Scarlet minivet

Macaws

Silk moth

Owl

Butterfly

Giant firefly

Box turtle

Piglets

Ants

Bat

Discus fish

Telescope goldfish

Hamster

Octopus

Sika deer

Toucan

Tiger

Discus fish

Cat

Rabbit

Treefrogs

Monarch butterflies

Tomato frog

Red crab

French bulldog

Blue-winged pitta

Killi fish

Dhole

Sika deer

Treefrog

Pufferfish

Tarantula

Clownfish

# Yellow

When wild animals are bright yellow, it attracts a lot of attention. Birds use this flashy shade to impress their mates, while insects and reptiles warn off predators. Darker yellows and golds are great for blending into deserts and dry grass, hiding local animals like lions from their prey.

Parakeets

Seahorses

Chicks

Fire salamander

Viper

Yellow weevils

Treefrogs

Crab spider

Banana slug

Bearded dragon

Python

Brain sponge

Yellow tang

Trevally fish

Butterflyfish

Land crab

Coal tit

Weaver bird

Wasps

Orange tip
butterflies

Box fish

Cane
toads

Snails

Lion cub

Golden
poison frog

Gold ram fish

Leopard gecko

Canary

Monarch butterflies

Sunbird

Butterfly

Corn snakes

Trumpet snails

Yellow tang

Ladybugs

Cheetah

Butterflies

Ducklings

Macaw

Emperor penguins

Parakeet

Crabs

Sun parakeet

Butterflies

Sea anemone

Treefrog

Grove snails

Python

Lion

Foxface rabbitfish

Axolotl

Labrador
retriever puppy

Butterflies

# Green

For hiding among leaves and undergrowth, green is the perfect disguise. It allows this little lizard to sneak up on juicy insects to eat. The insects don't see the lizard until it is too late.

Leaf mimic katydid

Scarab beetle

Damselfish

Red-eyed treefrog

Gecko

Butterfly

Grasshopper

Swallowtail caterpillar

Shining pot beetles

Egyptian green toad

Parrotfish

Crocodile

Treefrog

Butterfly

Butterfly

Flower beetle

Terrapin

Bearded dragon

Caterpillar

Mantis

Arboreal lizard

Lanternfly

Praying mantis

Green parrot

Parakeet

Chameleon

Parrotfish

Luna moth

Dead-nettle leaf beetle

Flower beetle

Butterfly

Grasshopper

Figeater beetles

Woodboring beetle

Dead-nettle leaf beetle

Machaon caterpillar

Caterpillar

Long-horned grasshoppper

Leafhopper

Beetle

Leaf insect

Fire-bellied toad

Leaf insect

Spinefoot fish

Hawksbill turtle

Green lizard

Beetle

Flower beetle

Butterfly

Tortoise

Chameleon

Cichlid

Lizard

Green shield bugs

Freshwater fish

Bee-eater bird

Hummingbird

Frog

Eastern tiger swallowtail caterpillar

Lanternfly

Festive Amazon parrots

Chameleon

Shining pot beetles

Red-crowned Amazon parrot

Lizard

Weevils

Green treefrog

Bamboo pit viper

Grasshoppers

Lovebirds

Spiders

Long-horned grasshoppers

Alexandrine parakeet

Weevils

Sapphira butterfly

Sunset moth

Bee-eater bird

Red-eyed treefrog

Iguana

Figeater beetles

Plumed basilisk

Red-eyed treefrog

Amazon parrot

Green treefrog

Australian green treefrog

Red-eyed treefrog

Rabbitfish

Blue-green chromis

Lanternflies

Iguana

Monkey grasshopper

# Blue

Blue is a color used for showing off on land, but in the sea it is used for blending in. The fish in this huge shoal match the blue of the water, making them difficult to count. Their enemies, such as sharks, find it tricky to pick them out to catch and eat.

Dart frog

Blue tits

Blue crayfish

Longhorn beetle

Violet beetle

Macaw

Blue-crested lizard

Woodboring beetles

Leaf beetles

Violet beetles

Jewelry beetle

Weevil beetles

Betta fish

Blue discus fish

Blue spotted fish

Powder blue tang fish

Tropical fish

Victoria crowned pigeon

Morpho
butterflies

Morpho butterfly

White-bellied redstart

Green sea turtle

Damselflies

Dragonfly

Sea slug

Sea slug

Sea stars

Blue-spotted
salamander

Peacock

Leaf
insects

Dung beetle

Unicornfish

Blue parrotfish

Electric eel

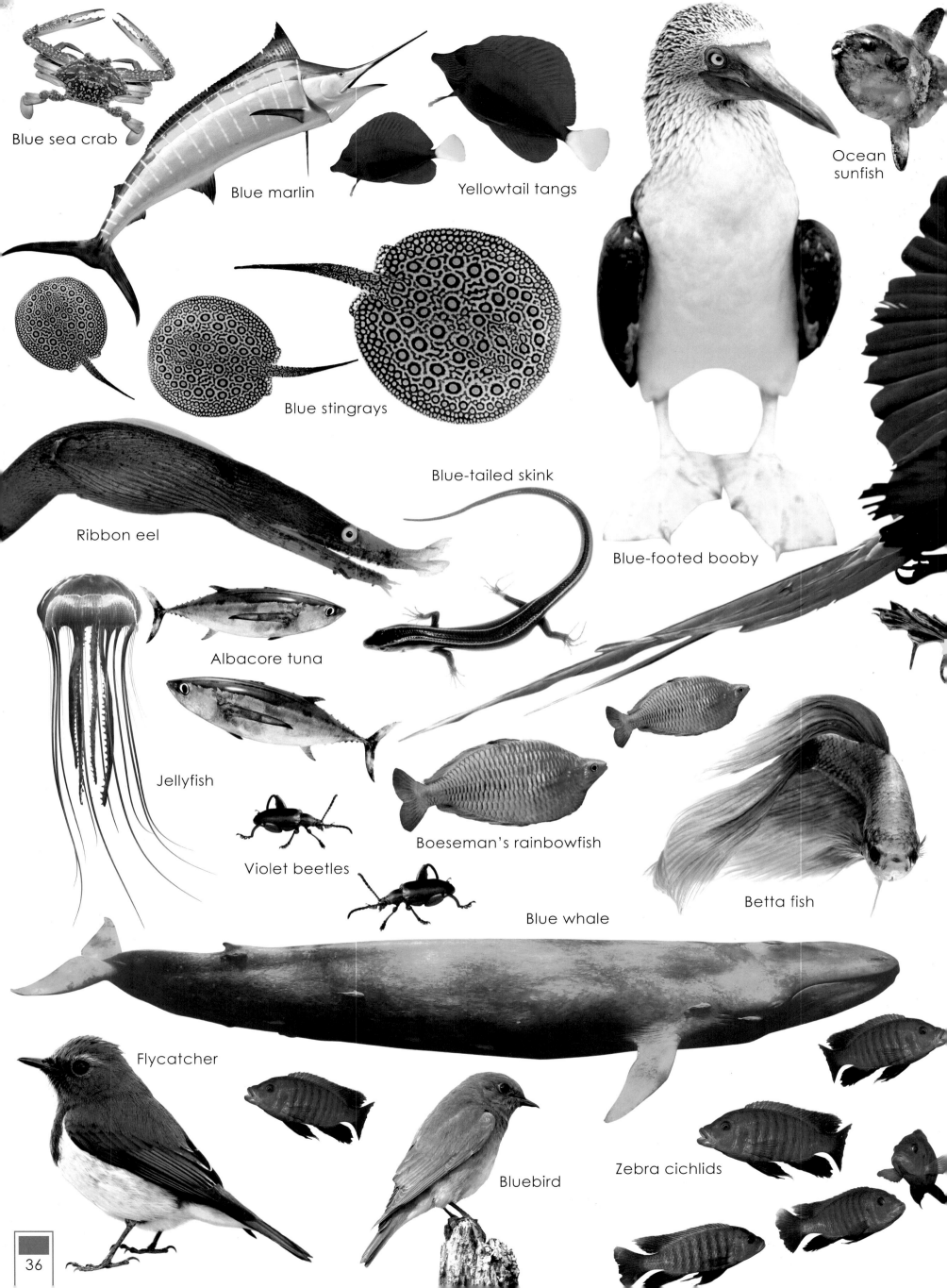

Blue sea crab

Blue marlin

Yellowtail tangs

Ocean sunfish

Blue stingrays

Blue-tailed skink

Blue-footed booby

Ribbon eel

Albacore tuna

Jellyfish

Violet beetles

Boeseman's rainbowfish

Betta fish

Blue whale

Flycatcher

Bluebird

Zebra cichlids

36

Common blue butterflies

Bluebird

Masked lovebird

Sea slug

Blue lobster

Macaw

Betta fish

Damselfly

Boxfish

Parrotfish

Betta fish

Betta fish

Black-crowned heron

Parrotfish

Bluejay

# Pink & Purple

A flock of pink flamingos is a beautiful sight. Flamingos are actually born with gray feathers. They get their pink color from the algae (tiny plants) and shrimps that they eat. This is true of many pink and purple birds.

Pink butterflies

Phasmatodea

Pink butterflies

Roseate spoonbill

Elephant hawk moth

Sphynx cat

Anthias

Pygmy seahorse

Sea stars

Orchid mantis

Japanese macaque

Sawfly larva

Flamingo

Flamingo

Pig

Sea mollusk

Scallop

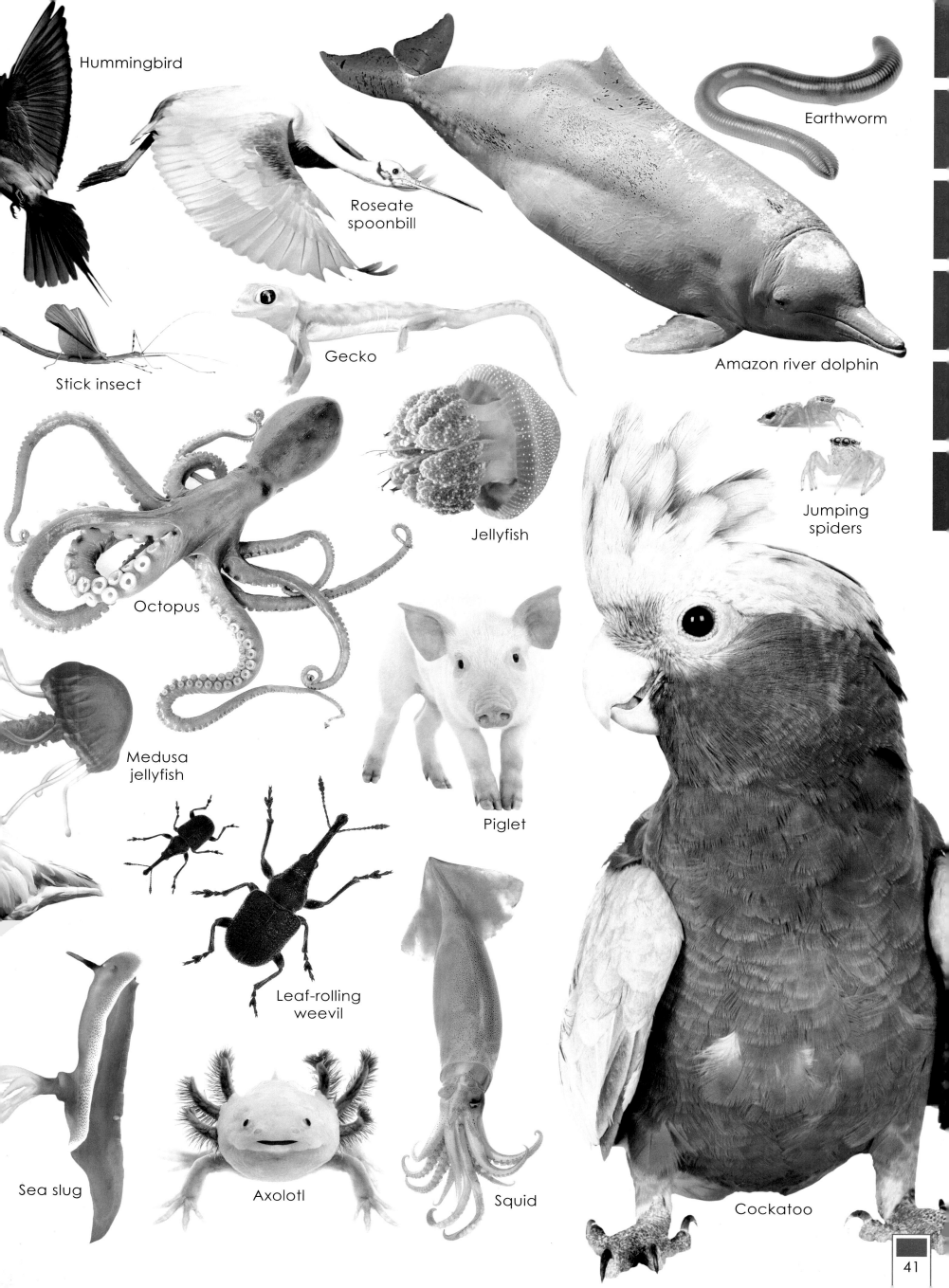

Hummingbird

Roseate
spoonbill

Earthworm

Stick insect

Gecko

Amazon river dolphin

Octopus

Jellyfish

Jumping
spiders

Medusa
jellyfish

Piglet

Leaf-rolling
weevil

Sea slug

Axolotl

Squid

Cockatoo

Bats

Butterfly

Octopus

Sunbird

Sand dollar

Humphead wrasse

Butterflies

Scarab
beetle

Sea urchin

Darkling beetle

Tropical fish

Yellowfin surgeonfish

Giant clam

Salamander

Hoopoe

Shiny
cowbird

Staghorn
coral

Hoopoe

Flatworm

Betta
fish

Sea stars

Poison dart frogs

Butterflies

Sea slug

Nautilus

Parrotfish

Hummingbird

Sea urchins

Tropical fish

Tropical fish

Scarab beetle

Brush-footed butterfly

Orchid mantis

Flatworm

Macaw

Butterflies

Blue tangs

Spanish shawl sea slug

Hummingbird

Dragonfly

# Brown

Animals that live in woods, deserts, or on the ground are often brown to blend in. It's tricky to spot the brown insects rushing around among these dead twigs and leaves.

Praying mantis

Bactrian camel

Silkmoth

Pheasant

Eagle owl

Wolf spider

Snail

Toad

Leafwing butterfly

Hedgehog

Katydid

Red deer

Greenbottle blue tarantula

Duck

Redknee tarantula

Stick insect

Grasshopper

Song thrush

Mantis

Owl

Russian tortoise

Caterpillar

Stag beetle

Rhinoceros beetle

Crested gecko

Red squirrel

Amazon tree boa

Diadem butterfly

Rabbit

Cricket

Pheasants

Amazonian
bush cricket

Millipede

Meerkat

Turkestan
cockroach

Red
kangaroo

Joey

Butterfly

Hedgehog

Giraffe

Brown bear

Box turtle

Scorpion

Grapevine
beetle

Moorish
gecko

Leaf
insect

Longhorn
beetle

Bush cricket

Mole cricket

Cricket

Arab mare
and colt

California
sea lion

Rabbit

Stink
bug

Red kangaroo

Gelbvieh bull

Eagle
owl

Llamas

Red setter

Penguin
chick

Steppe
eagle

Grizzly
bear

Red panda

Darkling
beetle

Chafer beetle

Caracals

Stag
beetle

Alpacas

White-tailed deer

Shetland pony

Fruit bat

Chow chow

Trout

Cricket

Orb weaver spider

Shield bug

Goat

Moth

Indian black antelope

Moth caterpillar

Leaf mimic katydid

Silkmoth

Cat

Viper

Wild boar piglet

Ants

Moorish gecko

Grapevine beetle

Centipedes

Sonoran desert toad

Snail

Orangutan

# Black, White & Gray

Zebras have stunning black-and-white coats. Their striking colors help to put off flies. It seems that the biting, blood-sucking flies don't like landing on the dazzling stripes. These stripes also confuse predators, by making it hard for them to see individual zebras within the herd.

Aquatic salamander

Scarab beetle

Grass snake

Horse

Scorpion

Butterfly

Tasmanian devil

Flower beetle

Angelfish

Transvaal girdled lizard

Labrador retriever

Dolphin

Giant anteater

Oil beetle

Southern ground hornbill

Black wildebeest

Fire-bellied newt

Egyptian cobra

Great mormon butterfly

Telescope goldfish

Rock monitor lizard

Mole

Indian bison

Sea urchin

Butterfly

Ant

Stag beetle

Red-tailed black shark

Skate

Minotaur beetle

Cat

Chimpanzee

Dog

Bess beetle

Angelfish

Armored beetles

Clownfish

53

American bison

Curlyhair tarantuala

Ferret

Giant snakehead fish

Leopard

Alpine newt

Peacock moth

Leaf beetle

Rhinoceros beetle

Butterfly

Minks

Italian mastiff

Giant Panda

Black moor goldfish

Humboldt penguins

Curlyhair tarantulas

Sea lion

Jackdaw

Black widow spider

Rook

Bonobo

Bald eagle

Rook

Horned beetle

Gorilla

Rooster

Magpie

Griffon vulture

Ferret

Orca whale

Sturgeon

Carpet beetle

Pot belly piglet

Llama

Earless seal

Stag beetle

Tamandua

Pyrenean
mountain dog

Rat

Humboldt
penguin

Alaskan
malamute puppy

Butterfly

Albino
American
alligator

Cabbage
butterflies

Snowy
owl

Hamster

Mute swan

English
bulldog

Tortoise beetle

Crowned
sifaka

Goat
and kid

Emperor
penguin

Maltese
puppy

Betta fish

Albino
deer

Ermine

Bigeye fish

White
lion

Fly
larvae

Albino
kangaroos

Hedgehog

Turkey

Cow

Caribou

Butterfly

Rat

Snow
leopard

Valais
lamb

Arctic fox

Flamingo

Stork

Gerbil

Arctic
fox

Coral

Brahman
calf

Saiga
antelope

Betta
fish

Albino ferret

Siamese kitten

Moth

Doves

Parrotfish

Capuchin monkey

Butterfly

Duck

Barn owl

Hedgehog

Albino kingsnake

Guinea pig

Pyrenean mountain dog

Butterfish

Chicken

Albino ball python

Bald eagle

Maltese puppy

Humboldt penguin

Fire goby

Jezebel
butterflies

Ermine

Kid

Snow leopard
gecko

Green
treefrog

Kid

Cockatoo

Crowned
sifaka

Gibbon

Fly lavae

Clown knifefish

Persian cat

Rabbit

Humboldt
penguin

Siberian husky puppy

Striped skunk

Rat

Sheep

Duck

Cabbage
butterfly

Giant
panda
cub

California
kingsnake

Oil beetle

Ant

White-backed vulture

Dove

Buzzard eagle

Sphynx kitten

Rabbit

Goose

Greater kudu

Giant anteater

Koala

Grey crowned crane

Owlet

Desert horned lizard

Komodo dragon

Warthog

Short-nosed unicornfish

Puffer fish

African grey parrot

Tapir

Puffer fish

Giant anteater

Otter

Sphynx cat

Scottish fold cat

Hippopotamus

Coypu

Weimaraner

Wolf

Chinchillas

Rat

Jackdaw

Seagulls

Macaque monkey

Short-nosed unicornfish

Verreaux's eagle-owl

African pompano

British shorthair cat

Tinselfish

Foureye butterflyfish

Cow

Andalusian horse

Kiwis

Tawny frogmouth

White rhinoceros

Rhinoceros

White-faced owl

Snowy owl

Clymene dolphin

Jackdaw

Aardvark

Pig

Arctic fox

Chinchillas

Cockatiel

Dwarf hamsters

Hawaiian gosling

Herring

Hippopotamus

Bottlenose dolphin

Raccoon

Whale shark

Pangasius

Stingray

Poodle

Bonnethead
shark

Cockatiels

Alligator
hatchling

Giant anteater

Heron

Rat

Raccoon

Ferret

African
grey parrot

Lop-
eared
rabbit

Wombats

Scottish
fold
kitten

Kangaroo

Komodo
dragon

African
elephant

Asian
elephant

Warthog

Florida
pompano

Rats

Japanese
macaques

Silver
barb

Mole

Tiger
shark

Sugar
glider

63

# multi-colored

Many animals are multicolored or have striking patterns. This allows them to hide from their enemies by matching patterns of light and shadows in nature, but can also be a way of standing out from the crowd.

Parrot

Chameleon

Chameleon

Red-eyed treefrog

Guppy

Pink-necked pigeon

Macaw

Parrotfish

Masked lovebirds

Banded pitta

Red-eyed treefrog

Clown triggerfish

Budgerigar

Mandrill

Sea slug

Peacock

Lorikeet

Blue-crested lizard

European bee-eater

Gouldian finch

Parakeet

Titan triggerfish

Spanish shawl sea slug

Sulawesi hornbill

Dung beetle

Butterfly

Hummingbird

Mandarin
duck

Lanternfly

Weevil

Jewelry
beetle

Treefrog

Spotted
sweetlips
fish

Woodboring
beetle

Macaw

Betta
fish

Woodboring
beetle

Blue tit

Mandarin
fish

Queen
angelfish

Kingfisher

Boeseman's
rainbowfish

Tropical fish

Butterflyfish

Betta
fish

Sun
parakeet

Hoeven's
wrasse

Poison dart frog

Comet

Egyptian green toad

Snowy owl

Stingray

Monkey grasshopper

Eastern baton blue butterfly

Dalmatian puppy

Sea slug

Pheasant

Asian water monitor

Gecko

Coral trout

Koi

Giraffe

Helmeted guinea fowl

Ladybug

Litchi bug

Hyena

Gecko

Speckled kingsnake

Pygmy seahorse

Coral trout

Cheetah

Stingray

Comet

Woodboring beetle

Spotted lady beetle

Harlequin sweetlips

Jaguar

Millennium gold discus fish

Asterope sapphira butterflies

Fire salamander

Butterfly

Stink bug

Snow leopard cub

Leopard

Butterfly

Longhorn beetle

Telescope goldfish

Scarab beetle

Black-head snake

Corn snake

Ladybug

Leopard slug

Grouper fish

Locust

Ladybug

Coral hind

Pigeon blood discus fish

Deer

Clown triggerfish

Weevil

Machaon
caterpillar

Jumping
zebra spider

Butterflyfish

Lemur

Emperor
angelfish

Lionfish

Redknee
tarantula

Clown
fish

Striped
shield bug

Snail

Bongo
antelope

Blue-crested
lizard

Centipede

Longhorn
beetle

Tiger
barb

Honey
bee

Zebra

Cat

Jewelry
beetle

Vulturine
guinea

Wasps

Woodboring beetles

Sea slug

Hungarian milksnake

Panther chameleon

White Bengal tiger

Snout beetle

Jewel scarab beetle

Checkered beetle

Oriental sweetlips

Striped spider

Woodpecker

Poison dart frog

Rosy boa

Caterpillar

Sugar glider

Bumblebee

Copperband butterflyfish

Clown surgeonfish

Zebra spider

Multibarred angelfish

Tiger

# Color Works

The three primary colors, red, yellow, and blue, can be mixed together to create all the colors of the rainbow. If you are lucky and you spot a rainbow in the sky, you will notice that the different colors blend into one another, creating a beautiful image in the sky.

In nature, animals most often match the colors around them, to stay hidden, but if they were all to come out and show off, they would make a magnificent living rainbow.

The next few pages explore different animals and their amazing colors. There is an animal for every color you can imagine! And even more, there are animals of every shade of every color. How many different blues can you count? How many more can you imagine?

Let these animal rainbows inspire you to notice all the colors in the world around you.

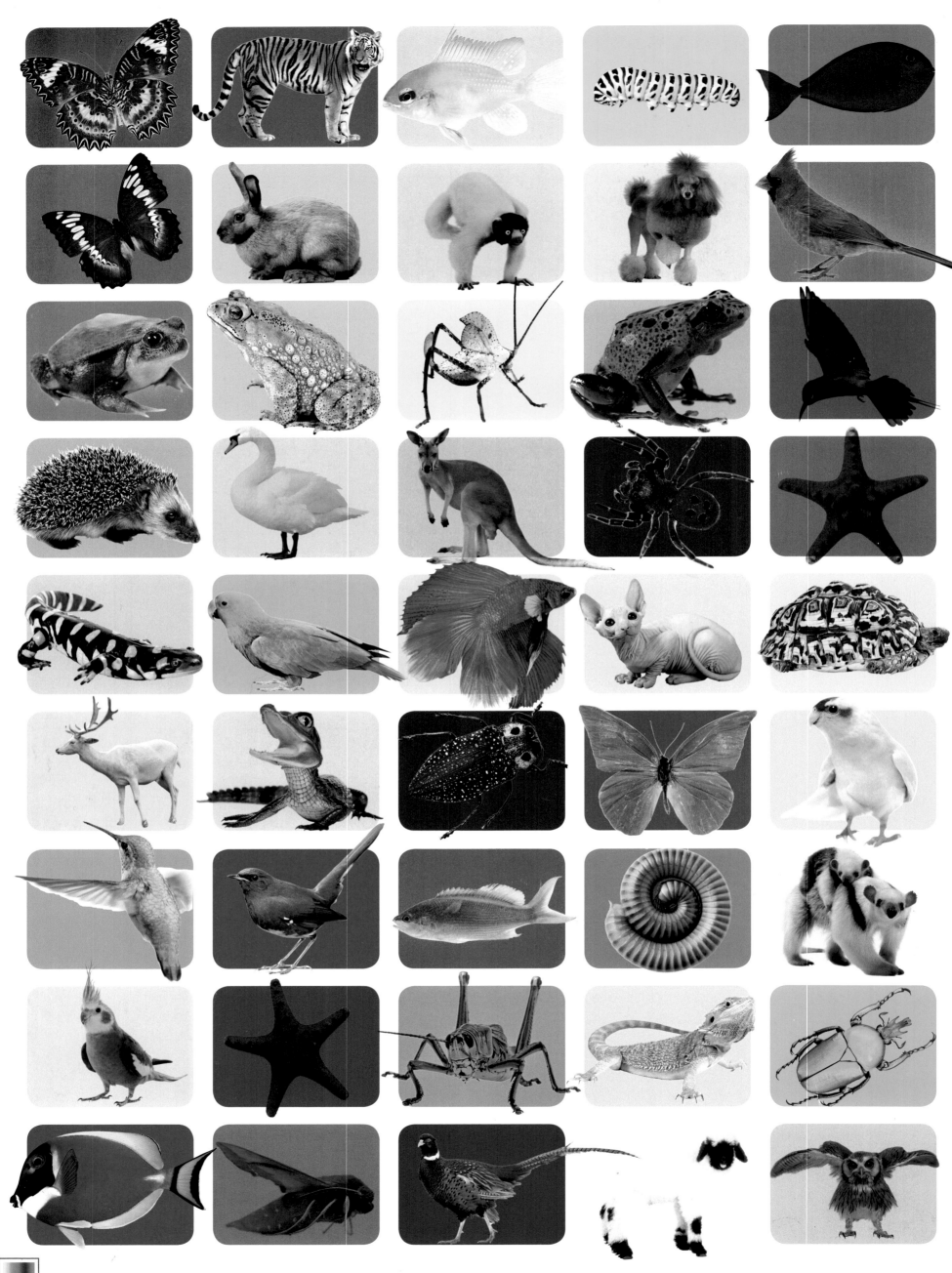

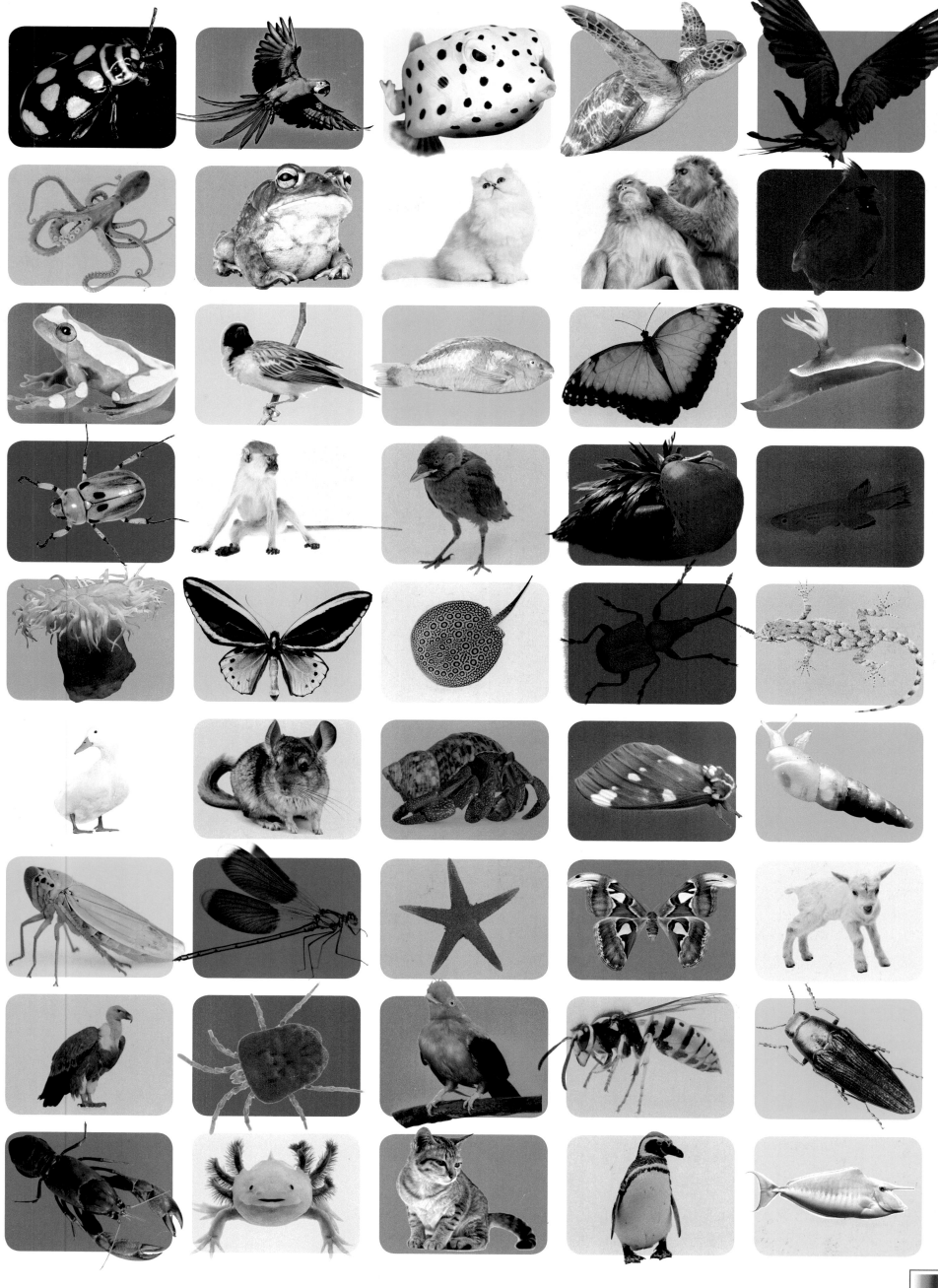

# Picture Credits

## Images used under license from Shutterstock.com.

### Photography Credits

**Page 1** Eric Isselee

**Page 2** Kasza; D and D Photo Sudbury; KAMONRAT; Brandon Alms

**Page 3** Kuttelvaserova Stuchelova; Aleksey Stemmer; prapass; Eric Isselee

**Page 4** Dushenina; Richard Whitcombe; Abeselom Zerit

**Page 5** nld; BOONCHUAY PROMJIAM; Africa Studio; Eric Isselee; phiseksit; Henrik Larsson; Marco Uliana; ANATOL; Marco Uliana; Lizard; Dr. Morley Read; stella_photo; kzww

**Hello Color** All images in this section have appeared and been credited in the appropriate individual color sections.

**Red** aaltair; Alik Mulikov; ANCH; Anton; Kozyrev; Boonchuay Promjiam; Butterfly; Hunter; Ch.L; Charles Brutlag; chiravan39; Dan Exton; Dirk Ercken; Dmitriy Kurnyavko; Dr. Morley Read; drpnncpptak; Edward Westmacott; Elena Schweitzer; Eric Isselee; eurobanks; fantom_rd; fivespots; halimqd; Hani Amir; Hhelene; irin-k; Jiang Hongyan; jiangdi; kamonrat; KanphotoSS; Krzysztof Odziomek; kzww; Melinda Fawver; Nataliya Taratunina; NinaMalyna; Nonnakrit; Olgysha; Paket; Patrick K. Campbell; Pedro Turrini Neto; pernsanitfoto; PeterVrabel; Protasov AN; Rich Carey; Rosa Jay; Schankz; Seashell World; serg_dibrova; Steve Heap; StevenRussellSmithPhotos; Susan Schmitz; Suttipon Yakham; tratong; tristan tan; Vladimir Wrangel; Voraorn Ratanakorn; Wiratchai Wansamngam; wong yu liang; Yellowj

**Orange** Africa Studio; Aleksey Stemmer; Anan Kaewkhammul; Andrey Armyagov; Asawinimages; Audrey Snider-Bell; Birdiegal; Brberrys; Butterfly Hunter; Chirtsova Natalia; Edward Westmacott; Ekaterina V. Borisova; Elizaveta Kirina; Eric Isselee; Ermolaev Alexander; Hugo Felix; jeep2499; Kazarlenya; Kletr; Lamyai; LeonP; Lotus Images; Lukas Gojda; Maksimilian; Marques; Matt Jeppson; Melinda Fawver; Mirko Rosenau; Monthira Yodtiwong; Nachaliti; Nantawat Chotsuwan; Natalia7; nattanan726; oksana2010; pan demin; phiseksit; photographyfirm; Rich Carey; Richard Peterson; Rosa Jay; skydie; Studio DMM Photography Designs & Art; sysasya; teekayu

**Yellow** Aleksandr Kurganov; Aleksey Stemmer; Andrew Burgess; BOONCHUAY PROMJIAM; Butterfly Hunter; Cameilia; CHEN WS; Cynoclub; Dr. Morley Read; Dray van Beeck; EEO; Eric Isselee; Fivespots; Friedemeier; Gonzalo Jara; GUDKOV ANDREY; Henrik Larsson; irin-k; Jag_cz; jeep2499; Johannes Kornelius; Kletr; Leksele; Lovely Bird; Mirko Rosenau; Pavel Hlystov; Pete Spiro; Piyathep; Potapov Alexander; prapat1120; Robert Eastman; Rosa Jay; Smit; suns07butterfly; tea maeklong; Volodymyr Krasyuk; wi6995; xpixel; yevgeniy11

**Green** Alexey Stiop; Alslutsky; aodaodaodaod; BlueOrange Studio; Bonnie Taylor Barry; Brandon Alms; boyphare; Cynoclub; digitalbalance; Donjiy; Dr. Morley Read; Eric Isselee; Fivespots; FotoRequest; Henrik Larsson; IamTK; Infografick; irin-k; Jiang Hongyan; Johannes Kornelius; Kamnuan; Kirsanov Valeriy Vladimirovich; Kletr; Kojihirano; Kuttelvaserova Stuchelova; Lawyerphoto; Le Do; Lindsey Eltinge; Lipowski Milan; Luis Carlos Jimenez del rio; Lukas Gojda; ManbettaTH; Marco Uliana; Medeia; Mr. SUTTIPON YAKHAM; Odua Images; Patryk Kosmider; Pichest; Prapass; Rosa Jay; Seiyoh; Sergey Dubrov; Smit; StevenRussellSmithPhotos; suns07butterfly; tratong; Ziga Camernik

**Blue** Aleksey Stemmer; Alistair Hobbs; Alslutsky; anat chant; Anna Baburkina; AnujinM; Bluehand; BOONCHUAY PROMJIAM; Brian Kinney; buttchi 3 Sha Life; cbpix; Cuson; Ehtesham; Ekaterina V. Borisova; Eric Isselee; Frolova_Elena; Guan jiangchi; Hans Gert Broeder; Holbox; James DeBoer; Kletr; Kosarev Alexander; Laszlo Csoma; Lodimup; Marco Uliana; Marques; Mike Truchon; MRCHARACTOR; Mrs_ya; Nantawat Chotsuwan; Napat; Nature Art; Nicola Dal Zotto; Oatfeelgood; Oshchepkov Dmitry; Pan Xunbin; Paul Brennan; Potapov Alexander; Rich Carey; Rosa Jay; serg_dibrova; Subbotina Anna; Super Prin; ZaZa Studio

**Pink** Agustin Esmoris; Anton_Ivanov; Butterfly Hunter; Coffeemill; cynoclub; Eric Isselee; Ethan Daniels; gopause; Hayati Kayhan; hsagencia; Igor Kovalchuk; Iurii Kachkovskyi; Jiri Vaclavek; Johannes Kornelius; Keyur Athaide; Luftikus; Marco Uliana; pan demin; panda3800; popox; Rich Carey; servickuz; smspsy; svetara; Svetlana Foote; Tapui; Tsekhmister; Vasca; ymgerman

**Purple** Aastock; alslutsky; BOONCHUAY PROMJIAM; Butterfly Hunter; Dobermaraner; Eric Isselee; Ethan Daniels; Fotyma; FUNFUNPHOTO; Giancarlo Liguori; Kajornyot; kamnuan; Karel Cerny; KENNY TONG; Kletr; Littlesam;

Maksim Shmeljov; Marco Uliana; mario pesce; NatalieJean; NattapolStudiO; Ondrej Prosicky; Phil Lowe; Potapov Alexander; ScubaPonnie; Seet; SeraphP; Servickuz; Super Prin; Tooykrub; zhengzaishuru

**Brown** Aaron Amat; Aksenova Natalya; Aleksey Stemmer; Alex Helin; Anton Gvozdikov; Anton_Ivanov; Aodaodaodaod; Aptyp_koK; Artush; Chinahbzyg; Cosmin Manci; D. Kucharski K. Kucharska; de2marco; disak1970; Dr. Morley Read; EEO; Eric Isselee; Ilikestudio; JIANG HONGYAN; Kirill Kurashov; Kletr; likhit jansawang; Liliya Kulianionak; Lizard; Luis Carlos Jimenez del rio; Luis Carlos Torres; Marco Uliana; Margo Harrison; Melinda Fawver; Mirek Kijewski; Natalia D.; Nelik; Olga_i; PAKULA PIOTR; Pandapaw; photomaster; Rosa Jay; Rsooll; Sarah2; Schankz; Smileus; Susan Law Cain; Susan Schmitz; Svetara; Tsekhmister; Vinne; Vitolga; YasenElena77

**Black** 2630ben; Luis Molinero; Makarova Viktoria; Marcin Pawinski; Marcin Perkowski; Matteo photos; merc67; Mike Price; MongPro; Montenegro; Mr. SUTTIPON YAKHAM; MR.Silaphop Pongsai; Napat; Natalia Fadosova; NATTHAPRAPHANIN JUNTRAKUL; Oleg Znamenskiy; Paul Looyen; Peter Waters; Photomaster; photosync; Rashid Valitov; Rebecca Tolman; Rosa Jay; Sascha Burkard; Sergey Uryadnikov; Skydie; SOMKKU; Somprasong Khrueaphan; Steve Boice; stockphoto mania; Super Prin; TatjanaRittner; think4photop; tristan tan; Tsekhmister; Ultrashock; Utekhina Anna; Viktoriia Bondarenko; Volodymyr Burdiak; WathanyuSowong; ZaZa Studio

**White** Africa Studio; Aleksey Stemmer; Alex Coan; Alslutsky; Anan Kaewkhammul; Andrey_Kuzmin; Anekoho; Anneka; Anton Kozyrev; ArtisticPhoto; Benny Marty; Bluehand; BOONCHUAY PROMJIAM; Butterfly Hunter; Camptoloma; carlos castilla; cgdeaw; chinnachote; Chris Howey; Christian Musat; Cosmin Manci; Couperfield; Cynoclub; cyran; D. Kucharski K. Kucharska; Danny Sullivan; Destinys Agent; Dien; Dja65; Dmitry Kalinovsky; Efendy; Elya Vatel; Eric Isselee; Evlakhov Valeriy; Fivespots; Foremostplus; Fotogiunta; FotoRequest; FotoYakov; Gallinago_media; Gopause; Hanphayak; Henrik Larsson; Iakov Filimonov; Ibrahim Buraganov; Ilya D. Gridnev; Inna Astakhova; Iurii Kachkovskyi; jeep2499; Jeffrey B. Banke; JIANG HONGYAN; Jim H Walling; Johann Helgason; Johannes Kornelius; Jorge Felix Costa; Joy Tasa; K.A.Willis; Kamnuan; Kletr; Krasowit; Kuznetsov Alexey; Kwangmoozaa; Lena Pan; Luca De Gregorio; Mariocigic; Maros Bauer; Matt Antonino; NattapolStudiO; Nipastock; oksana2010; Oleksandr Lytvynenko; Onur ERSIN; Pan Xunbin; Peter Waters; Photomaster; Praisaeng; Robert Eastman; Robynrg; Rosa Jay; Sbolotova; Sebastian Gora Photography; Serg Rajab; Shchipkova Elena; suns07butterfly; thirayut; Tischenko Irina; Tom Bird; Top Photo Engineer; Valery Plotnikov; WilleeCole Photography; www.BillionPhotos.com; xpixel

**Gray** Anan Kaewkhammul; AndreJakubik; Andrew Burgess; Andrey Burmakin; Anton_Ivanov; Anyamay; Bachkova Natalia; Benny Marty; Cameilia; cbpix; Couperfield; Cynoclub; DJ Mattaar; Ekaterina V. Borisova; Eric Isselee; Evgenyi; Evlakhov Valeriy; FotoRequest; Gwoeii; Hintau Aliaksei; HunterKitty; Iakov Filimonov; Ilonika; IrinaK; jassada watt; Kirill Vorobyev; Kletr; Korionov; Luis Carlos Jimenez del rio; Lukas Gojda; Mariait; MARKABOND; MeePoohyaMeePhoto; Mr. SUTTIPON YAKHAM; Nrey; oksana2010; otsphoto; photolinc; photosync; Potapov Alexander; Ralf Juergen Kraft; Raymond Thill; Reinhold Leitner; Scorpp; SF photo; Sonsedska Yuliia; Talvi; Toloubaev Stanislav; Tsekhmister; Zawafoto; ZaZa Studio

**Multicolored** 2630ben; Aaron Amat; Akil Rolle-Rowan; Aleksey Stemmer; Allocricetulus; Alslutsky; Ana Vasileva; Andamanec; Anton Kozyrev; Aodaodaodaod; asawinimages; bluehand; BOONCHUAY PROMJIAM; Borislav Borisov; Brandon Alms; Butterfly Hunter; Cameramannz; Cbpix; Christian Delbert; Coffeemill; DAE Photo; Denis Tabler; EcoPrint; Ehtesham; Eric Isselee; Ermolaev Alexander; Fivespots; Frolova_Elena; FUNFUNPHOTO; Gopause; Iakov Filimonov; IamTK; irin-k; jaroslava V; Jim H Walling; Johannes Kornelius; Kamnuan; Kletr; Kosarev Alexander; Lisa Charbonneau; Maksimilian; Marco Uliana; Mike Truchon; Mirek Kijewski; Mirko Rosenau; Monkeyoum; Monthira Yodtiwong; Nantawat Chotsuwan; Napat; NatalieJean; nattanan726; Nature Art; Nekrasov Andrey; Neophuket; Nrey; Olgysha; panda3800; Panom Pensawang; Panu Ruangjan; Pedro Turrini Neto; Phant; Photographyfirm; photomaster; Praisaeng; Prapass; prapat1120; r.classen; Rich Carey; Rosa Jay; Sakdinon Kadchiangsaen; Seiyoh; serg_dibrova; Sergey Tsvetkov; Somprasong Khrueaphan; stella_photo; Super Prin; Susan Schmitz; TatjanaRittner; Tom Willard; tristan tan; Vaclav Volrab; Valery Plotnikov; volkova Natalia; Volodymyr Krasyuk; Worraket; www.BillionPhotos.com; yothinpi

**Color Works** All images in this section have appeared and been credited in the appropriate individual color section.

**Page 80** Oleg Elena Tovkach

All photographs in this book including those used on the cover and jacket are used under license from Shutterstock.com with the following exceptions:
page 10, "Crab" ©chiravan39/iStock
page 36, "Pygmy Blue Whale" ©Franco Banfi/naturepl.com

While every effort has been made to credit all contributors, Weldon Owen would like to apologize should there have been any omissions or errors, and would be pleased to make any appropriate corrections for future editions of this book.